INDIANAPOLIS
COLTS

by Brian Peloza

Published by ABDO Publishing Company, 8000 West 78th Street, Edina, Minnesota 55439. Copyright © 2011 by Abdo Consulting Group, Inc. International copyrights reserved in all countries. No part of this book may be reproduced in any form without written permission from the publisher. SportsZone™ is a trademark and logo of ABDO Publishing Company.

Printed in the United States of America,
North Mankato, Minnesota
062010
092010

Editor: Chrös McDougall
Copy Editor: Nicholas Cafarelli
Interior Design and Production: Christa Schneider
Cover Design: Craig Hinton

Photo Credits: David Drapkin/AP Images, cover; NFL Photos/AP Images, title page, 19, 23, 25, 26, 29, 42 (bottom), 43 (top); David Duprey/AP Images, 4; Kevork Djansezian/AP Images, 7; Chris Carlson/AP Images, 9; Jeff Roberson/ AP Images, 10; Amy Sancetta/AP Images, 13, 43 (middle); AP Images, 14; John Rous/AP Images, 16, 42 (top); Harold Matosian/AP Images, 20, 42 (middle); Andrew J. Cohoon/AP Images, 31; George Widman/AP Images, 33; Adam Nadel/ AP Images, 34; Lenny Ignelzi/AP Images, 37; Stephan Savoia/AP Images, 38; Ben Liebenberg/AP Images, 41, 43 (bottom); Darron Cummings/AP Images, 44; Tom Strickland/AP Images, 47

Library of Congress Cataloging-in-Publication Data
Peloza, Brian, 1977-
  Indianapolis Colts / Brian Peloza.
    p. cm. — (Inside the NFL)
  ISBN 978-1-61714-014-3
  1. Indianapolis Colts (Football team)—History—Juvenile literature. I. Title.
  GV956.I53P45 2010
  796.332'640977252—dc22
                                2010017023

TABLE OF CONTENTS

CHAPTER 1

WINNING BIG

For Peyton Manning and the Indianapolis Colts, the 2006 season opener was special. The Colts' opponent that day was the New York Giants. Their quarterback was Eli Manning. It was the first National Football League (NFL) game in which two brothers started at quarterback.

Older brother Peyton got the best of this contest. The Colts defeated the Giants 26–21 at Giants Stadium in East Rutherford, New Jersey. That historical start was just one of many highlights for Colts' fans during the 2006 season. After beating the Giants, Indianapolis went on to finish 12–4 during the regular season. The Colts then won three playoff games to qualify for Super Bowl XLI.

The Super Bowl was a chance for Peyton Manning to prove his critics wrong. Throughout his career, he had been known as one of the league's top quarterbacks. He had already set a handful of passing records in his career. In 2004, he even threw for a then-record

PEYTON MANNING AND THE COLTS HAD TO BATTLE RAIN AS WELL AS THE CHICAGO BEARS IN SUPER BOWL XLI.

RECORD-SETTING YEAR

Indianapolis set several team and league records during the 2006 season. Quarterback Peyton Manning set the team record for completions in a win over the Houston Texans on September 17, 2006. Johnny Unitas held the previous record of 2,796. Manning also extended his NFL record to nine straight seasons with more than 25 touchdown passes.

Wide receiver Marvin Harrison set an NFL record with 159 consecutive games with a reception to start a career. Later in the season, Harrison caught his 115th touchdown pass, passing Lenny Moore for the team lead in total touchdowns scored.

Coach Tony Dungy and Manning won their fifty-sixth game together after beating the New England Patriots on November 5, 2006. They broke the team record set by former Baltimore Colts coach Don Shula and Unitas.

49 touchdowns. However, some people believed he was unable to win in a big game. Manning and the Colts would have to battle more than just the Chicago Bears to do it, though.

Super Bowl XLI was played in Miami, Florida. The game was scheduled there because Miami usually has nice weather in February. But on this day, a heavy rain fell as the teams took the field to start the game.

The Bears came into the game with one of the top defenses in the league. Many expected their defense to be even more effective in the rain. That is because the Colts played their home games in the RCA Dome. Since domes provide perfect playing conditions, they are an ideal setting for high-flying offensive teams. The Colts definitely fit that

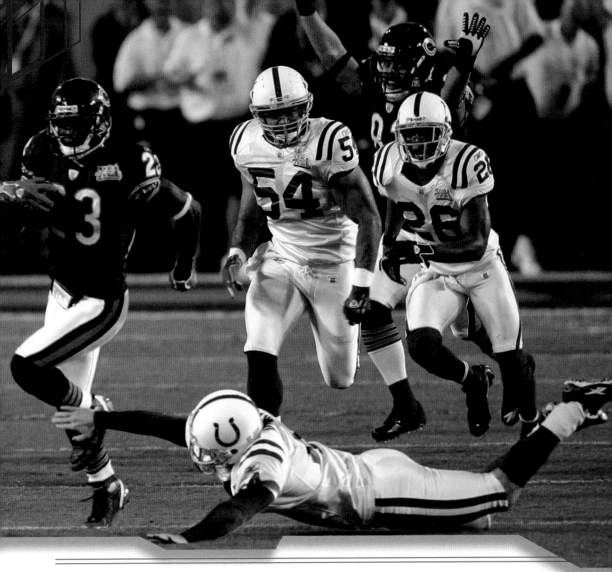

COLTS KICKER ADAM VINATIERI COULD NOT STOP BEARS KICK RETURNER DEVIN HESTER ON THE OPENING PLAY OF SUPER BOWL XLI.

description. They had tied for the NFL lead in passing touchdowns and were second in passing yards during the 2006 regular season. Now Manning would have to lead the Colts in very imperfect conditions.

The game got off to a terrible start for the Colts. Chicago rookie Devin Hester returned the opening kickoff 92 yards for a touchdown. Then Manning was intercepted on the Colts' first possession.

The Colts finally got a break on their next possession. Manning found wide receiver Reggie Wayne for a 53-yard touchdown. However, the rain caused the Colts' holder to drop the snap for the extra point.

The sloppiness continued. Both teams had three turnovers

in the first half. Even the Colts' reliable kicker Adam Vinatieri missed a field-goal attempt in the second quarter. The rain did not let up in the second half. But neither did the Colts. They slowly took control of the game. Going into the fourth quarter, they held a 22–17 lead.

The Bears began a drive early in the fourth quarter. A touchdown would have given them the lead. Even a field goal would have made the game uncomfortably close for the Colts. Instead, an unlikely Colts' player stepped up.

Second-year cornerback Kelvin Hayden had been an unheralded draft pick out of the University of Illinois. But on the fourth play of the Bears' drive, Hayden intercepted a pass from Chicago quarterback Rex Grossman. He then returned it 56 yards for a touchdown.

MR. CLUTCH

Kicker Adam Vinatieri is no stranger to pressure moments in the Super Bowl. Prior to joining the Indianapolis Colts in 2006, he won three Super Bowls with the New England Patriots. Vinatieri kicked game-winning field goals to clinch two of those Super Bowl wins.

Vinatieri's 48-yard field goal as time expired lifted New England past the St. Louis Rams, 20–17, in Super Bowl XXXVI. His 41-yard field goal with four seconds remaining gave the Patriots a 32–29 win over the Carolina Panthers in Super Bowl XXXVIII.

INDIANAPOLIS CORNERBACK KELVIN HAYDEN INTERCEPTS A CRUCIAL PASS IN THE FOURTH QUARTER OF SUPER BOWL XLI.

"I was just thinking about getting into the end zone," Hayden said. "We stepped up the whole postseason where we just made the plays and the defense buckled down."

The Colts held on to win Super Bowl XLI 29–17.

There had been many key individual efforts in the game. Rookie running back Joseph Addai rushed for 77 yards on

19 carries. He also caught 10 passes for 66 yards. Backup running back Dominic Rhodes rushed 21 times for 113 yards and one touchdown. Vinatieri kicked three field goals in the game. His 49 points that post-season set an NFL record.

In the end, it was Manning who was the biggest star. Despite the poor conditions, Manning completed 25 of 38 passes for 247 yards and a touchdown. For his effort, Manning was named the game's Most Valuable Player (MVP). He had finally won—and thrived in—the biggest game.

The Colts' coach also cemented his place in history that day. Tony Dungy became the first African-American head coach to win a Super Bowl.

Winning a Super Bowl was not new for the Colts franchise. The Colts had beaten the Dallas Cowboys to win Super Bowl V in 1971. However, that was when the team was located in Baltimore, Maryland. It relocated to Indianapolis in 1984.

Super Bowl XLI was special because it was one for the city of Indianapolis to call its own. The city also had a team of hardworking players who were easy to

AN ELITE GROUP

Quarterback Peyton Manning put himself in rare company by leading the Colts to a win in Super Bowl XLI. He became one of four quarterbacks to be drafted with the first overall pick and later win in his first Super Bowl appearance.

Troy Aikman did the feat with the Dallas Cowboys in Super Bowl XXVII. Jim Plunkett (Oakland, Super Bowl XV) and Terry Bradshaw (Pittsburgh, Super Bowl IX) preceded Aikman and Manning in accomplishing the feat.

COLTS ROOKIE RUNNING BACK JOSEPH ADDAI HAD 143 YARDS OF TOTAL OFFENSE IN SUPER BOWL XLI.

REWRITING THE RECORDS

Peyton Manning has turned the Colts' record book into his own career stat line. Manning owns every top-10 mark for single-season completions, attempts, and yards. Manning completed 392 of 591 pass attempts during the 2002 season, both single-season records. His 4,557 passing yards in 2004 is a team record.

The only significant passing category in which another quarterback appears in the top 10 is single-season touchdown passes. Johnny Unitas's 32 touchdown passes in 1959 still rank third in team history.

However, Manning holds all of the rest of the spots in the top 10 in that category, too. Manning's 49 touchdown passes in 2004 was an NFL record until it was broken by New England Patriots quarterback Tom Brady's 50 three years later.

cheer for. One day after Super Bowl XLI, Dungy was at the team's rally at the RCA Dome. There, he recalled a meeting he had with Colts' President Jim Irsay while interviewing for the job.

"[Irsay] said, 'I want you to win a Super Bowl,'" Dungy said. "We decided that was what we're going to set out to do, but we also said one other thing. We said we're going to win one the right way. We're going to win with great guys, we're going to win it with class and dignity, and we're going to win it in a way that would make Indianapolis proud.

"I think we've accomplished that."

PEYTON MANNING ADMIRES THE VINCE LOMBARDI TROPHY AFTER GUIDING THE COLTS TO VICTORY IN SUPER BOWL XLI.

CHAPTER 2

WINNING EARLY AND OFTEN

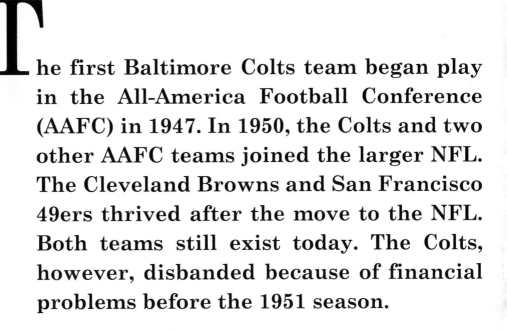

The first Baltimore Colts team began play in the All-America Football Conference (AAFC) in 1947. In 1950, the Colts and two other AAFC teams joined the larger NFL. The Cleveland Browns and San Francisco 49ers thrived after the move to the NFL. Both teams still exist today. The Colts, however, disbanded because of financial problems before the 1951 season.

Behind strong local support, Baltimore soon got a second chance to have a professional football team. The NFL awarded the city a new team in 1953. This team replaced the Dallas Texans, who folded the season before. The new team was also named the Colts. The name paid tribute to the city's rich history in horse racing.

The new Colts team picked up where the old team left off: losing. In fact, the new team had a losing record in each of its first

JOHNNY UNITAS, *LEFT*, AND COACH WEEB EWBANK GUIDED THE BALTIMORE COLTS TO MANY SUCCESSFUL SEASONS.

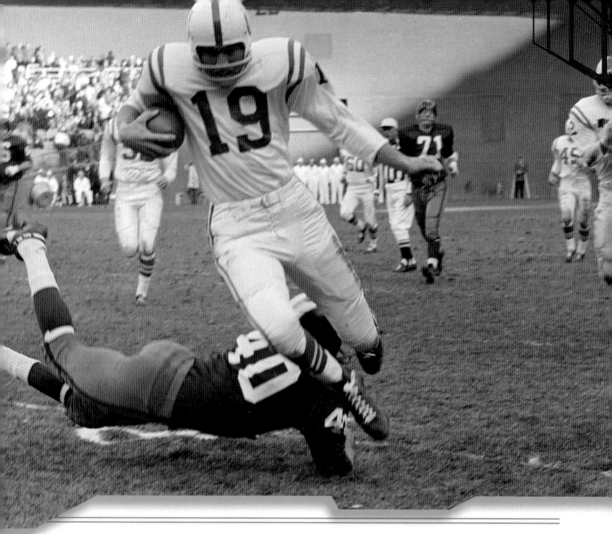

COLTS QUARTERBACK JOHNNY UNITAS RUNS FOR A GAIN DURING A 1963
GAME AGAINST THE WASHINGTON REDSKINS.

four seasons. But when the Colts hired Weeb Ewbank as head coach in 1954, a brighter future at least looked possible.

Ewbank slowly but surely added talented players to the Colts' roster. The team slowly improved under Ewbank, too. After going 3–9 in 1954 and 5–6–1 in 1955, the Colts finished 5–7 in 1956. More important than the 1956 record, however, was the emergence of rookie quarterback Johnny Unitas. The

1956 season would be the last losing season the Colts would experience for several years.

Unitas had guided the team to a 3–4 record in seven starts as a rookie. He greatly improved during his second season. The Colts finished the 1957 season with a record of 7–5. That began a streak of 15 consecutive nonlosing seasons in Baltimore.

Unitas led the Colts all the way to the NFL Championship Game after the 1958 season. The Colts played against the New York Giants at Yankee Stadium in New York City. A national audience watched on television. At the time, it was the most-watched game ever. The fans picked a good one to follow. The exciting, back-and-forth action came all the way down to the end of regulation.

CHANGING THE GAME

Tight end John Mackey achieved success early in his career. He was even selected to the Pro Bowl as a rookie in 1963. Mackey was the only first-year player selected to play in the 1963 all-star game.

During his career, Mackey transformed the way coaches looked at the tight end position. His speed allowed the Colts to use him as a pass-catching threat and not just a blocker. In 1966 he had nine touch-down receptions, including six scores of more than 50 yards.

Mackey spent nine of his 10 seasons with the Baltimore Colts before finishing his career with the San Diego Chargers. He caught 331 passes for 5,236 yards in his career.

Mackey was enshrined in the Pro Football Hall of Fame in 1992. At the time, he was just the second tight end in the Hall.

In the final two minutes, Unitas led the Colts 73 yards down the field. Colts kicker Steve Myhra hit the game-tying field goal with seven seconds left. The teams went to sudden death overtime. That meant that the first team to score would win.

The Colts stopped the Giants on the first possession of overtime. Then, Unitas took over once again. He led the Colts 80 yards down the field on 13 plays. The Colts then secured the win when fullback Alan Ameche scored on a 1-yard touchdown.

Many consider the contest to be the "greatest game ever played." Professional football took off in popularity in the years following the game.

The Colts returned to the NFL Championship Game after the 1959 season. They once again faced off against the Giants. Unitas led the Colts with two passing touchdowns and one rushing touchdown. With their 31–16 win, the Colts successfully defended their NFL title.

Ewbank had helped build the Colts team. However, he would not finish his career there. Ewbank left the Colts after the 1962 season to coach the New York Jets of the American Football League (AFL).

Ewbank became the only coach to win championships with teams from both the NFL and the AFL. He would later come back to be a thorn in the side of the Colts, too. However, in 1963, Baltimore was more concerned

COLTS FULLBACK ALAN AMECHE (35) IS SLOWED BY NEW YORK GIANTS
DEFENSIVE BACK JIMMY PATTON IN THE 1958 NFL CHAMPIONSHIP GAME.

with finding a new head coach.
The team decided to go with
33-year-old Don Shula. He
became the youngest head coach
in NFL history. Decades later,
he would retire as one of the
best ever.

THE PACESETTER

*Johnny Unitas was the first NFL quarter-
back to throw for 40,000 career yards.
Since then, 10 other quarterbacks have
passed that mark. Those quarterbacks
include Brett Favre, Dan Marino, John
Elway, Peyton Manning, Warren Moon,
Fran Tarkenton, Vinny Testaverde, Drew
Bledsoe, Dan Fouts, and Joe Montana.*

CHAPTER 3

MAINTAINING EXCELLENCE

Under Don Shula, Baltimore returned to the NFL Championship Game once more, following the 1964 season. However, this game was much less memorable than the previous ones. The Colts were shut out 27–0 against the dominant Cleveland Browns.

Beginning in 1966, the NFL champion began playing the AFL champion in what later became known as the Super Bowl. The Colts played in their first Super Bowl following the 1968 season.

Unitas only played in five games during that season because of an elbow injury. However, backup Earl Morrall played so well that he was named the NFL MVP. Heading into Super Bowl III, the Colts were heavy favorites against the AFL's New York Jets.

Jets star quarterback Joe Namath had other ideas, though. Before the game, he "guaranteed" that the Jets would win. Weeb Ewbank, who was

COLTS PLAYERS CARRY COACH DON SHULA OFF THE FIELD AFTER THE TEAM WON THE 1964 NFL WESTERN DIVISION TITLE.

coaching the Jets, said he "could have shot him," for making the guarantee. Few people believed the AFL could compete with the NFL at the time. The Colts were also coming off a dominant 13–1 regular season.

Namath lived up to his word, though. He led the Jets to a 13–0 fourth-quarter lead. In desperation, an injured Unitas came out and tried to save the game for the Colts. He passed for

their only touchdown, but it was not enough. The Jets won 16–7.

Shula guided the Colts to a 73–26–4 record during his seven years with the team, including playoffs. However, he was unable to win a Super Bowl. He left to coach the Miami Dolphins beginning in 1970.

Under a new coach, Don McCafferty, the Colts went 11–2–1 in 1970 and reached their second Super Bowl. They played the Dallas Cowboys. Unitas threw a 75-yard touchdown pass in the game. The ball actually bounced off one Colts receiver and then a Cowboys defender before John Mackey pulled it in and ran for the touchdown. However, Unitas later had to leave the game due to injury.

The Colts and Cowboys combined for 11 turnovers in Super Bowl V. However, the final score

PERFECTION

Don Shula showed much promise during his time in Baltimore. However, his greatest coaching achievements came after he left to coach the Miami Dolphins. In 1972, Shula coached the Dolphins to a 14–0 regular-season record followed by a victory in Super Bowl VII. That 1972 Dolphins team remains the only team ever go undefeated through the regular season and then win the Super Bowl. By the time Shula retired after the 1995 season, he was the winningest coach in NFL history with an all-time record of 347–173–6 (including playoffs).

OFFENSIVE TACKLE BOB VOGEL WALKS OFF THE FIELD DURING THE COLTS' 16–7 LOSS TO THE NEW YORK JETS IN SUPER BOWL III.

was not determined until the very end. With 7:35 left, Baltimore's Tom Nowatzke rushed for a 3-yard touchdown to tie the game at 13–13. Then linebacker Mike Curtis intercepted Cowboys quarterback Craig Morton and returned it to the Dallas 28-yard line.

With five seconds remaining in the game, Baltimore kicker

PRICE OF WINNING

When Baltimore won Super Bowl V in 1971, each player on the Colts earned a $15,000 bonus. In comparison, when the Indianapolis Colts won Super Bowl XLI in 2007, each member of the Colts earned a $73,000 bonus.

BRINGING A CROWD

The Colts had many future Hall of Fame players during their run of success in the 1950s and 1960s. They included wide receiver Raymond Berry, running back/receiver Lenny Moore, tight end John Mackey, defensive linemen Art Donovan and Gino Marchetti, and offensive lineman Jim Parker. However, Johnny Unitas was the ultimate star of the Baltimore Colts. He was inducted into the Pro Football Hall of Fame in 1979.

Unitas also headlined a group of Colts players who were named to the NFL's fiftieth anniversary team in 1969. A group of 36 Hall of Fame voters selected the team. The first team also included Mackey and Marchetti. Berry and Donovan made the second team, while Moore made the third team.

Of playing with Unitas, Mackey said, "It's like being in a huddle with God."

Jim O'Brien hit a 32-yard field goal. The Colts had won their first Super Bowl 16–13.

The winning ways in Baltimore would not last, however. After 17 years with the Colts, Unitas was traded to the San Diego Chargers in 1973. When he retired after the 1974 season, he held 22 NFL records. His never-before-seen passing skills had changed the NFL forever. In his career, Unitas completed 2,830 of 5,186 pass attempts for 40,239 yards and 290 touchdowns. His streak of 47 consecutive games with a touchdown pass still stands.

"Johnny Unitas is the greatest quarterback ever to play the game, better than I was, better than Sammy Baugh, better than anyone," said Pro Football Hall of Fame quarterback Sid Luckman.

LEGENDARY COLTS QUARTERBACK JOHNNY UNITAS, SHOWN IN 1970, WAS INDUCTED INTO THE PRO FOOTBALL HALL OF FAME IN 1979.

The team won three straight division titles in 1975, 1976, and 1977 with Ted Marchibroda as the head coach. However, the Colts' combined record over the next five years was 19–53–1.

After Super Bowl V, the Colts would not win another playoff game until 1995. By then, they would no longer be the Baltimore Colts.

CHAPTER 4

MOVING DAY

On March 28, 1984, Colts owner Robert Irsay approved a secret mission. In the middle of the night, 15 green and yellow Mayflower moving trucks showed up at the Colts' Baltimore training complex. The movers packed up all of the team's things and drove away into the snowy night. The Colts were moving to Indianapolis, Indiana.

The move came as a shock to Colts fans. Irsay had been at odds with the local government and news media for some time. But as people speculated about whether he would try to move the team, Irsay had promised to never do that. The fans felt betrayed when the team left. However, they were even more irked about how it happened: in secret, during the middle of the night.

William Donald Schaefer was Baltimore's mayor at the time. He had initially defended

CENTER RAY DONALDSON AND THE COLTS KICKED OFF IN INDIANAPOLIS, INDIANA, STARTING IN 1984.

Irsay when people began questioning if Irsay would move the team. Then, the Mayflower trucks showed up.

"In a way, this gets very personal to me, when I thought someone would at least pick up the phone and say to me 'I'm going,'" he said. "I'm trying to retain what little dignity I have left in this matter. If the Colts had to sneak out of town that night, it degrades a great city."

Many former Baltimore Colts fans are still sour over the move to this day. However, the city did get a new team in 1996 when the Cleveland Browns became the Baltimore Ravens.

An open house at the team's new facility in Indianapolis drew 10,000 visitors. When season tickets were offered, there were 143,000 inquiries in two weeks. However, many people from Indiana felt guilty over how they got an NFL team. It took many years before the people there truly accepted the team as their own.

Wins were rare for the Colts during their early seasons in Indianapolis. They won a total of only 12 games during their first three seasons after the

NOT ME

With the first pick in the 1983 NFL Draft, the Baltimore Colts selected quarterback John Elway out of Stanford University. There was one slight problem. Elway did not want to play for Baltimore. He forced the Colts to trade him, which the team did. Elway was traded to the Denver Broncos for quarterback Mark Herrmann, offensive lineman Chris Hinton, and a first-round draft pick in the 1984 NFL Draft. Elway went on to win two Super Bowls with the Broncos.

COLTS RUNNING BACK ERIC DICKERSON CARRIES THE BALL DURING THE 1987 PLAYOFFS. INDIANAPOLIS LOST 38–21 TO THE CLEVELAND BROWNS.

move. The Indianapolis Colts had their first winning record in 1987. That was partially due to the addition of star running back Eric Dickerson.

The Colts started the season 0–2. Their third game was cancelled due to a player strike. The team then won two of their next three games with replacement players. The regular players rejoined the team for Week 6. They traded for Dickerson before

TRADING FOR A HALL OF FAMER

The Indianapolis Colts made a big trade during the 1987 season that brought running back Eric Dickerson to town. He was immediately successful. Dickerson rushed for 1,659 yards during the 1988 season. He became the first Colts player to lead the league in rushing since Alan Ameche did it in 1955. Dickerson played three more seasons with the Colts. He finished his career with stops with the Los Angeles Raiders and the Atlanta Falcons. Dickerson rushed for 13,259 yards in his career and was inducted into the Pro Football Hall of Fame in 1999.

Week 7. The Colts won six of the nine games Dickerson played in that season. They finished 9–6 and won the American Football Conference (AFC) East Division title. However, they lost to the Cleveland Browns 38–21 in the playoffs.

It was not until 1995 that the Colts got to experience the postseason again. Ted Marchibroda took over as the team's head coach in 1992. He had coached the Colts from 1975 to 1979 when they were in Baltimore. Along with a man nicknamed "Captain Comeback," Marchibroda guided the Colts to a 9–7 record that year.

Quarterback Jim Harbaugh was called "Captain Comeback" because he rallied the Colts to several come-from-behind victories. In Week 2, the Colts fell behind the New York Jets 24–3 in the third quarter. Harbaugh

COLTS RUNNING BACK MARSHALL FAULK RUNS PAST NEW ORLEANS SAINTS DEFENDER RUFUS PORTER EN ROUTE TO A TOUCHDOWN IN A 1995 GAME.

came off the bench and led the Colts to a 27–24 win. Later that season, Harbaugh helped the Colts make up a 21-point deficit against the Miami Dolphins. The Colts scored 21 straight points in the second half and ended up beating the Dolphins 27–24 in overtime.

RUNNING WILD

Running back Marshall Faulk proved to be a force for the Colts during his brief stay with the team. He was named to three Pro Bowls during his time in Indianapolis, which lasted from 1994 to 1998. Faulk rushed for 1,000 yards in four of his five seasons with the Colts. Faulk finished his career with the St. Louis Rams. He played seven seasons and won a Super Bowl with the Rams.

"These guys had the kind of faith in Jim that the Cowboys have in Troy Aikman, that the Dolphins have in Dan Marino, that the Steelers had in Terry Bradshaw," said Colts vice president Bill Tobin. "They get in the huddle and know something good is going to happen."

Following the 1995 regular season, the Colts won their first playoff game since Super Bowl V. In fact, they won two playoff games. The Colts beat the San Diego Chargers 35–20 in the first round. They then beat the Kansas City Chiefs 10–7. Their string of good fortune ran out in a game against the Pittsburgh Steelers, however. The Colts lost 20–16 in the AFC Championship Game.

The Colts were unable to build their success from the 1995 season into another Super Bowl appearance. They went 9–7 in 1996 but lost in the second round of the playoffs. In 1997, the Colts struggled to a 3–13 record.

Although the Colts were not always fun to watch during that 1997 season, all of that losing did pay off. Since they had the worst record in the league, the team got the top pick in the 1998 NFL Draft. With that selection, the Colts would change the future of their team.

A LONG TIME COMING

In 1995, Colts rookie running back Zack Crockett rushed for 147 yards on 13 carries in a 35–20 win over the San Diego Chargers in the AFC playoffs. Crockett scored on touchdown runs of 33 and 66 yards in the game. He set a team record for rushing yards in a playoff game. At the time, Crockett was one of 12 players on the team who was not even born the last time the Colts won a playoff game.

"CAPTAIN COMEBACK" JIM HARBAUGH LED THE COLTS BACK TO THE AFC CHAMPIONSHIP GAME AFTER THE 1995 SEASON.

CHAPTER 5

CREATING A DYNASTY

With the first pick in the 1998 NFL Draft, the Indianapolis Colts selected quarterback Peyton Manning. He had been a star quarterback at the University of Tennessee. His father, Archie Manning, had been a star quarterback for the New Orleans Saints during the 1970s. With Peyton, the Colts now had a superstar player to build their team around for many years to come.

With Manning and new coach Jim Mora, the Colts had high hopes for the 1998 season. Manning played well as a rookie. He threw for 3,739 yards and 26 touchdowns. He was even named to the all-rookie team. However, the Colts finished a lowly 3–13.

Since that losing season, Manning and the Colts only had one losing season through 2009. The Colts won 115 games from 2000 to 2009. That made them the winningest team in the NFL during the decade.

THE COLTS SELECTED PEYTON MANNING FROM THE UNIVERSITY OF TENNESSEE WITH THE FIRST PICK OF THE 1998 NFL DRAFT.

Much of the Colts' success during that time has been because of their high-powered offense. The Colts had selected wide receiver Marvin Harrison in the first round of the 1996 draft. Manning and Harrison connected for 112 touchdowns in their years playing together. That is the most ever by a wide receiver-quarterback tandem. Manning also had star receiver Reggie Wayne and star tight end Dallas Clark to pass to during much of that time.

Manning quickly became known for having one of the strongest and most accurate throwing arms in the NFL. However, he did not always need to pass. The Colts selected running back Edgerrin James with their first-round draft pick in 1999. In seven seasons with the Colts, he was selected to four Pro Bowls. His replacement in 2006, Joseph

QUITE THE START

Quarterback Peyton Manning is the only player in NFL history to start his career with 12 consecutive seasons of 3,000 passing yards. He owns 12 of the 18 3,000-plus passing yard seasons in team history. John Unitas and Bert Jones each accomplished the feat three times. Manning has been rewarded for his excellence by being selected to 10 Pro Bowls. He has also been named NFL MVP on four occasions—2003, 2004, 2008, and 2009.

Addai, was selected to the Pro Bowl in 2007.

Despite having a dominant offense, the Colts were unable to reach a Super Bowl during Manning's early years. Mora had helped turn the Colts into a winning team. But to take the next step the team believed it needed somebody else.

The Colts fired Mora after the 2001 season. The Tampa Bay Buccaneers had fired their coach, Tony Dungy, around the same time. As it turned out,

PEYTON MANNING HANDS THE BALL OFF TO EDGERRIN JAMES DURING A 2004 GAME. MANNING AND JAMES PLAYED TOGETHER FOR SEVEN YEARS.

Dungy was the perfect fit to take over in Indianapolis.

"He was by far the best candidate out there," Colts owner Jim Irsay said. "Tony is a proven winner and an ideal type leader who we want to represent the horseshoe."

SCORING MACHINE

The Colts ranked near the top of the NFL offensive statistics throughout Peyton Manning's career. Through 2009, the Colts ranked among the top four scoring teams in eight of the previous 11 seasons. The Colts led the AFC in passing six times in 11 seasons. Indianapolis also ranked in the top 10 in total offense among all NFL teams in 10 of the past 11 seasons.

WIDE RECEIVER MARVIN HARRISON CELEBRATES A TOUCHDOWN AGAINST THE NEW ENGLAND PATRIOTS IN 2006.

One of Dungy's first tasks was to fix the Colts' defense. Indianapolis had allowed more than 30 points per game during the 2001 season. Even their second-ranked offense could not make up for that. The Colts were 6–10 during Mora's last season.

"We'll get our defense fixed, and we'll be even better on offense," Irsay said. "Tony gives us a chance to be better sooner. I am convinced he gives us the best chance to win the Super Bowl. When you consider Tony Dungy, the man, and Tony Dungy, the perfect fit for this organization, no way was I going to let this get away."

Irsay was right. Just four seasons after Dungy came to Indianapolis, the Colts won Super Bowl XLI by defeating the Chicago Bears 29–17.

The Colts' defense steadily improved during the 2000s. Much of that was due to the additions of star players like defensive end Dwight Freeney and safety Bob Sanders. However, the Colts' success always started with Manning and the offense. He was on pace to break nearly every NFL passing record at that decade's close.

Through the 2009 season, Manning had thrown 366 touchdown passes. That ranked third all-time, behind Brett Favre and Dan Marino. Manning was

EPIC RIVALS

Throughout the early and mid-2000s, the Indianapolis Colts and the New England Patriots played in many epic games. Part of the reason these games drew so much interest was because of the quarterbacks. Many people considered Colts quarterback Peyton Manning and Patriots quarterback Tom Brady to be the two best quarterbacks of their generation.

Manning often put up better stats than Brady. However, in the big games, Brady always seemed to win. The Patriots beat the Colts in the 2003 AFC Championship Game and the 2004 playoffs. In February 2005, Brady won his third Super Bowl title.

The tide finally turned in 2006. With about two minutes left in the AFC Championship Game, the Colts trailed the Patriots by three points. Manning then led the Colts 80 yards down the field for a touchdown. The Colts won 38–34. Two weeks later, they beat the Bears in Super Bowl XLI.

also near the top in career passing yards. In addition, he had thrown 25 touchdown passes in a record 12 consecutive seasons.

The Dungy era came to a close in Indianapolis after the 2008 season. His long-time assistant Jim Caldwell replaced him. Caldwell got off to a very fast start. The Colts won their first 14 games of the 2009 season. Some people thought they could have gone undefeated, but the team played many backups in its final two games and lost both. Still, Manning won his fourth NFL MVP award after the season.

In the playoffs, the Colts rolled through the Baltimore Ravens and then the New York Jets. They finally met their match in Super Bowl XLIV. The New Orleans Saints capped off their best season ever with a 31–17 victory over the Colts.

Even though the Colts did not win their second Super Bowl since moving to Indianapolis, their winning tradition continued. With Manning leading the way, Colts fans are optimistic that their team will be back at the Super Bowl again soon.

IRONIC TWIST

The Colts won an NFL-record 23 straight regular season games over parts of the 2008 and 2009 seasons. The winning streak was snapped in a 29–15 loss to the New York Jets at home. The Colts were ahead 15–10 late in the third quarter when rookie Curtis Painter replaced Peyton Manning at quarterback. The Colts pulled Manning to make sure he would be healthy for the playoffs. The Jets took advantage and ended up winning the game. It is not the first time the Jets gave the Colts a stinging defeat. The Jets defeated the Colts in Super Bowl III, a game that many consider one of the greatest upsets of all time.

PEYTON MANNING THROWS TO A RECEIVER IN SUPER BOWL XLIV. AFTER AN AMAZING SEASON, THE COLTS LOST TO THE SAINTS 31–17.